BIOGRAPHICAL SKETCH

OF

JOHN EVANS,

DEPUTY GOVERNOR OF PENNSYLVANIA,

WITH

LETTERS FROM THE PROPRIETOR, WILLIAM PENN, NOW FIRST PRINTED.

BY

THE REV. EDWARD D. NEILL,
PROVOST OF JESUS COLLEGE AT THE FALLS OF SAINT ANTHONY, MINNESOTA.

Reprinted from the NEW-ENGLAND HISTORICAL AND GENEALOGICAL REGISTER for October, 1872.

BOSTON:
PRINTED BY DAVID CLAPP & SON.
1872.

BIOGRAPHICAL SKETCH OF JOHN EVANS.

JOHN EVANS was of Welsh extraction, the son of Thomas Evans, of London, who had been a seafaring man, an old friend of William Penn "who loved him not a little."

He was about twenty-six years of age when he was commissioned as lieutenant governor of Pennsylvania. The proprietor, in a letter to the secretary of the province, in 1703, alludes to his appointment in these words:—

"He shows not much, but has a good deal to show, and will gain upon the esteem of the better sort. He has travelled and seen armies, but never been in them. Book learning as to men and government he inclines to; carries over some good books, and expects among mine and thine to help himself with more. Give him as soon as he comes a hint of persons and things and guide his reading."

He did not profess to be a member of the society of Friends, and Richard Hill, a Quaker, described him as "an Episcopal man, young and solid."

Accompanied by William Penn, Jr., the surviving son of the first wife of the proprietor, he reached Philadelphia on 11th day 12th month, 1703–4. Isaac Norris wrote to a friend: "The Governor and William Penn, Jr. caught us napping, arrived late last night."

Norris had come to Philadelphia from Jamaica, stood high in the society of Friends, and was a solid and intelligent merchant. From respect to the proprietor, and a love of hospitality, he was willing to receive young Penn into his family, although his wife had the care of "six children small and tender."

Evans lodged at first with a Mr. Paxton, and then at Sheriff Finney's, but the habits of both of the young gentlemen were such that respectable housewives soon felt that their absence was more agreeable than their presence.

James Logan, the virtuous and scholarly secretary of the province, always anxious to serve the proprietor and to preserve the dignity of the province, at length rented for a government house the great brick, double front mansion of lawyer William Clarke. It was considered the most splendid residence in the city, and stood in capacious grounds at the corner of Third and Chestnut streets, facing the latter and also Dock creek. Here were gathered as fellow-boarders — Penn, Evans, and Mompesson; the latter had been a member of parliament and recorder of Southampton, now a judge of the province, subsequently chief-justice of New-York. Logan gave them the best rooms, and, to use his own language, "turned up into the garret," preferring, no doubt, the retirement of an humble attic with his classical books to the bacchanalian orgies of the lower floors.

Not many weeks elapsed, before the three inmates of Clarke Hall became the town talk. At a late hour one night, there was a riot in a tavern, kept by one Enoch Story, in which young Penn and Gov. Evans were participants. It is said that Penn called for pistols, and that the lights being blown out, a city alderman "availed himself of the darkness to give Evans a severe drubbing."[1] Evans, on the other hand, about this time is alleged to have called into a tavern and there flogged a constable named Solomon Cresson.[2]

Penn was indignant at being arraigned before the mayor's court, and was afterward more intemperate. About this time Lord Cornbury, son of the Earl of Clarendon, visited Philadelphia and with his wife was handsomely entertained by young Penn at Pennsbury, the country seat of the proprietor. After this, Penn determined to return to England by way of New-York, Byerly, collector of the customs there, agreeing to loan him money.

Norris, writing to a friend, says: "William Penn, Jr., is quite gone off from Friends. He being in company with some extravagants that beat the watch at Enoch Story's was presented with them. * * * * He talks of

[1] Watson's *Annals*, ed. of 1830, p. 101.
[2] Hazard's *Register*, vol. iv. p. 112.

going home in the Jersey man-of-war next month. I wish things had been better, or he had never come."

The following letter to his friend Evans was written before he sailed.

[WM. PENN, JR., to LT. GOV. EVANS.]

N. York 8br 18th, 1704.

DR SR,

The Hurry I have been in, in preparing for my voyage has been ye only occasion of my not writing sooner, but I could not omitt this opportunity wth ou^t assuring yow How much I (wth ou^t a Compliment) your Humble servant. I hope if I can serve you, you will not scruple to command me, nobody shall be a more faithful friend. God Prosper you in all your undertakings and make ye People ——— and Happy.

Your very Hum^ble friend,
WM. PENN, JR.[1]

What is amiss,
Pray impute to our
way of living Here—

There was no improvement upon the part of the governor after his friend's departure. He was self-important, and "had more of the rake in his character than of any thing else."[2]

On one occasion he met a countryman coming to town with a heavily loaded wagon. He ordered the man to halt and allow him to pass by. The teamster being slow in his movements, with a louder voice he repeated the demand with threats. The countryman now roused, in not very nice

[1] William Penn, Jr., was the surviving son of Penn's first wife, Gulielma Springett. Before he came to America he had married Mary Jones. Logan wrote to his father: "'Tis a pity his wife came not with him, for her presence would have confined him within bounds he was not too regular in observing." To pay his debts and return to England he was obliged to sell his manor, now the site of Norristown. Penn wrote to Evans in 1705 of his son: "He is like to be somebody here in a while I think." But the father's hopes were never realized. His intemperate habits increased. Leaving his family in England he went to France and died there in 1720, from the result of dissipation, two years after his father's decease.

His widow was a foolish, extravagant woman, and Hannah, the second wife of the proprietor, once wrote that she wished "she had brought more money since she had brought so little wisdom to help the family."

The children of William Penn, Jr., were: Gulielma Maria, Springett and William. The grandfather, in his letters of 1703, speaks of "my grandson Springett a mere Saracen, his sister a beauty." In another he calls the infant William, "the little Billy, the spark of them all." This William died in 1746. He married first, Miss Forbes, then after her death, Ann Vaux. His daughter married Mr. Gaskill, whose descendants are living in Pennsylvania.

[2] Extract from Smith MSS. *New-Jersey Historical Society Proceedings*, vol. viii. p. 131.

language, asked "Who he was, that being *on foot*, wanted a cart with a heavy load to turn out for him?" He answered, "I am the governor." The countryman rejoined by saying "he lied, for the governor was more of a gentleman, and had more consideration," and began to ply his whip upon the person that he felt was an impostor. At length the wagoner discovered that every governor was not a gentleman, and that he had assaulted Governor Evans, and with humble apologies escaped from the awkward dilemma into which he had been forced by the churlishness of Penn's representative.

The Quakers were opposed to even defensive war. They believed that if they never used, they would never need the sword. The encroachments of the French, and the growing hostility of the Indians, clearly demanded a militia organization, and Evans, soon after his arrival, began to form military companies.

As the Quakers were slow to respond to his plans, he resorted to a "boyish trick" to frighten them into his measures. By his instigation, a letter came to the sheriff of New-Castle with the forged name of Seymour, governor of Maryland subscribed, stating that a French fleet was approaching, and requesting that Governor Evans be immediately informed. The unsuspecting sheriff instantly despatched a messenger to Philadelphia, and the letter reached Evans while dining on the banks of the Schuylkill, at the residence of a Mr. Roche, "a generous liver," lately from Antigua. Hurrying to town, the governor convened the council, and read the letter to them with the solemn face of one who believed that every statement was as true as Holy Writ. The result was the issuing of a proclamation requiring all persons to furnish themselves with arms and ammunition, and for two nights the militia were on duty. During the excitement he rode about town with drawn sword, urging people to bear arms. Many of the unsuspecting citizens, fearing the approach of the French, fled from town, others hid their valuables in wells or buried them in their cellars.

The next step of the governor was still more impolitic, well stigmatized by Penn as "an extreme false step." He insisted that all vessels passing the fort at New-Castle, should pay a duty of one half pound of powder for each ton of burden. The merchants of Philadelphia resisted the exaction and complained to the proprietor, who considered the free and undisturbed passage of ships up and down the Delaware river a fundamental right of the charter of the province.

In the year 1708, without the knowledge of Secretary Logan, he gave Michel,[1] a Swiss adventurer, a permit to mine toward the sources of the Potomac, and made the proprietor believe that there were great prospects. William Penn, deep in debt, harassed by creditors, neglected by those whom he had befriended, was excited by the thought that he might through a silver mine replenish his fortune, and he clung to the expectation as a drowning man clings to a straw. In a letter to Logan, dated from London, 29 day 7 mo. 1708, he says: "Pray go to the bottom with Colonel Evans about the mines, and what has become of Michel? Who are let into the secret? Where are they? Who have worked them? It is a test upon J. Evans's honour and regard to me. I take his story (if he stays) to be a proof he believes it and stays to benefit himself."

Logan in reply said: "There is yet nothing certainly discovered about the mines. Col. Evans has been very free with me upon that head. There has been none opened, and I heartily wish I may be able to tell thee more of the matter hereafter, for I fear Michel has tricked us all. He has gone over to England with an intention we believe of putting his countrymen, the Swiss, upon purchasing a tract beyond the Potomac."[2]

The private life of Evans was as censurable as his public conduct. Shunning the company of the correct and judicious Logan,[3] the secretary of the province, he for a time lived in an obscure house near the northern suburbs of the city. He had a liaison with one Susan Harwood, whose mother had escaped out of a debtors' prison, to which Penn alludes in deep

[1] Michelle, or Mitchell, afterwards settled, with other Swiss, in New Berne, North Carolina.

[2] *The Friend,* vol. xix. p. 122.

[3] Logan thus complains about Evans not paying his board, in a letter to the proprietor: "After Master William had been here a few months lodging at Isaac Norris' we became so troublesome to his numerous family that we were obliged to remove and take a house. The lieutenant-governor first took lodgings at A. Paxton's, when his [Paxton's] wife's health rendering his stay improper, he removed to John Finney's, whence in a little time he was obliged to look out again, but finding no place, and I considering that we were already at the charge of housekeeping, and that wherever he went till money were otherwise raised, I must answer it on thy account, concluded therefore to invite him to the same house, as it was in general thought most proper.

Upon which to give way to him I turned up into the garret. Thy son departing in a few months after, we were left to keep house by ourselves. When we first entered on it I told Master William I could bear no other part than to pay as a boarder, that at Isaac Norris' I paid £30 per annum, and at another's £20 for a servant, and that here I would allow £60 per annum but would no more."—*Friend,* vol. xviii.

sorrow in one of the appended letters. When he was removed from office he was a good deal surprised, and "broke his intended match with J. Moore's beautiful daughter,"[1] and the continuing of improvements upon a plantation he had obtained near New-Castle on the Brandywine, but it was ultimately renewed, and on the 28th 8 mo., 1709, he married the "fair Reb. Moore," the daughter of the advocate of the admiralty court, and until he left America kept house in the then fine Fairman mansion, near the treaty tree.

His successor, as deputy-governor, was Charles Gookin, about 48 years of age, whose grandfather, Sir Vincent Gookin, was nearly related to Daniel Gookin, who as early as 1620 sent cattle from Ireland to Virginia, and came himself in 1621, settled at Newport News, and whose son Daniel became the friend of the Indian missionary Eliot, died in 1687, and was buried in Cambridge, Mass.[2]

Penn had known the Gookin family in Ireland for forty years, and Charles, who had served in the army and had a soldier's religion,"[3] had been highly recommended as a successor to Evans by the Ingoldsby family and Generals Earle and Cadogan. Although not a free-liver he was eccentric, failed as an executive officer, and bore himself like a martinet.

Watson states that he sent for one of the judges and kicked him because he would not grant his wish. This and other strange conduct created the impression that he was partially deranged.

Evans, after surrendering his office to Gookin, remained for a time in Philadelphia, but at length retired to Denbigh, Wales. In November, 1716, he purchased of his former companion, young William Penn, 2000 acres of the manor of Steyning on Brandywine creek, and the following March gave John Moore, his father-in-law, power to sell the same;[4] but in 1731, as John Evans, of Pentry Manor, co. Denbigh, he declares before a master in chancery that he never authorized Moore to sell any land.[5]

His daughter Mary married a Dr. Barry, and her great-grandchild, an

[1] Logan correspondence, in *Friend*, 1846.

[2] For genealogical information relative to the Gookin family, see REGISTER, vol. i. pp. 345–52; vol. ii. pp. 167–74; vol. iv. pp. 79–82 and 185–8.

[3] Penn to Logan.

[4] Deed-Books, Philadelphia.

[5] Catalogue of Benjamin Coleman, London, July, 1870.

Irish maiden lady, gave the writer the originals of two of the following letters, and allowed him to copy the others that follow.

[William Penn to Lt.-Gov. Evans.]

Coll. Evans London 5th of ye 7m (Mar.) 1704.
Esteem'd ffr'd

It is now neer six months Since you sayl'd from Spithead, and not ye least intimation yet arriv'd as of your getting well to your Journey's end, which makes all uneasy. We understood by ye master of one of yr fleet yt was carried into Martineco by a French Privateer & was deliver'd by one of our ships takeing ye Privateer in his way to France, that you were all well, ye ffleet I mean, ye 2 of Xbr being four days after our unexampled storme yt has more than taxt ye nation 4ss in ye pound by ye divastations it has occasioned.

My tax is 30lb where I live but I have sustained about fifty, & am come off more than equall with ye best. But you will have the Prints to tell you all. It seems America the Continent at least had a mighty Tempest on ye 7th of 8br, while you were upon yr voyage, but the winds of neither side made themselves knowne, that to this, or this to y side of the world.

I hope thyn & my son's arrivall have contributed to ye quelling that which has so long agitated the people of my Governm't—I shall say nothing of their unfairness to make the want of things a reason of Complaint & then hinder supplying that want by secretly discourageing the means used to answer it, as wt my Depty Goverr did about Capitall Cases, trying men for life by oath, and the Militia, which one Bantifeux harrangu'd so clamorously about & reggistring of vessels upon oath only since thy arrivall & approbation will putt an end to all those things.

Positively stand to ye letter of ye pow'rs of my Patent, whatever orders come from hence yt I know nothing of, or thos fractious Spirits do, or say there. Without resolution as well as meekness & Patience there is no Good; wherefore keeping within the Compass of the Laws of ye Province & powrs of my Grant fear nothing, while I am here & able to follow my own business; I hope by this opertunity to send you a letter, or at least to get one sent, or a coppy thereof from ye Lords Comrs for Trd & Plants in reproof C. Quarry's Insolence to address, wth his vestry Lord Cornberry a Guest in our own town & Goverm't, Civilly invited and treated, to write to the Queen to take our Goverm't away from us, an Imprudence yt is without precedent, & for wch he deserves ye severest rebukes & discountenance.

I must tell thee, I am much more like to keep my Goverm't than to sell or loose it, & therefore am not upon those uncertain and precarious Circumstances they hope yt are my enimys & our fr'ds may fear; ffor our great men plainly see ye motives of these folks to vex us & more resolve to support us in our just rights, and to less vallue the clamour ag'st us. But pray take care of Trade & Queen's Revenue and then feed y^m wth good hard meal y^t with softer treatment will be Insolent or disorderly to Goverm't.

Thy mother sent to-day to see me & I have dispatcht one to her business, C. Puckler being gone to-day & I going out of Town at 3 this afternoon. C. L.[1] thinks to write to thee and my son, now, or by way of N. York: intending then my resentm't to y^t Lord, of Quarry's business.

John, lett honour, conscience, and old friendship prevaile to acquit thyselfe to me & my family and the Country according to our Laws and Constitution, not yet repeal'd, till they are so, in a legal manner wch as yet is farr off. My son and daughter salute y^e & so does with good wishes

Thy true ffriend,

Wm. Penn.

P. S. I can say no more till I heare from thee of the state of things. Be just and then wise. Salute me to ye Councill and Magestrates—Farewell. W. P.

Thy Mother's business was only to hear of thy wellfare.

[From the Same to the Same.]

Bristoll 6 9bre 1704.

Esteemed Friend

I cannot let this Bearer goe without a salutation (for it is by another hand in ye same ship that I have writ to thee already but 'tis about 6 weeks if not two months agoe.

ffirst thy relatives were lately well to whom I took care to deliver thy letters; thy uncle is now or lately was on his circuit & in Cornhill. I have given thy salutes to L'd Clarendon &c. and the character I have had of thy conduct, and with them, has done thee service.

I can make no Judgem't of our affaires, only that the adverse Interests struggle mightily and 'tis thought this session of Parliament will issue it one way or t'other.

Our affaires in Germany in a secure condition, not so in Portugall & yet worse in Savoy, but ye other successes more than Ballance y^t & some think that y^t war is but begun. Vast preparations on both sides.

I have both thine, as in a former I intimated, I only desire thee steer legally by Just interest, and w'^{t} room there is for favour to be on ye side of my affaires; for If I keep my Gov'rm't, thou keepest my Lieftenantcy and If I resigne, one article will be to continue thee there, for it will be hardly done, but by consent.

As I would have thee just to all, so discreet to our enemys, but kinde to ye ffriends of ye Country, & of my honest interest. I have hinted at large to ye Secretary, my

[1] Charlewood Lawton, Penn's lawyer.

minde about ye division of ye up'er and lower countys, and let James Coutts know whatever they can desire of thee as my Dept I shall acquiesce in what thou does upon thy best consideration, and those of ye Province that one of ye worthiest mindes, and further confirme the same notwithstanding the ungratefull and unworthy behaviour of Rob't ffrench & John Hill.

Lett W. Clarke[1] know pray that I have his, per last opertunity, and have his former, and writ an answeare. Tell him I shall complain to ye Comrs of Trade & Plantations about ye Marylanders, and consider of ye rest he writt of.

I need not bid thee respect my Son & yet I would not carry yt too farr, and I hope there will be no need of it. Thy ff'ds remain such. I wish I could say the same. If it lays in thy way to help ye bearer pray do, he is a poor kinsman of my wife's, who salutes thee, as does with a true regard

Thy Sincere &
affect. ffriend
WM. PENN.

My salutes
to ye Council & Magistrate
& ye well inclined at large.

[FROM THE SAME TO THE SAME.]

London 30th 7, 1705.

COLL. EVANS &
Esteemed Frd.

Thy last was of the 5th month last, in haste, So Short, chiefly intimating the hasty coming over of Coll. Quary. I hope he has no Com'issions from our ungrateful crew on that Side the water, the unwearied troubler of our poor Israel, and here are our Pennsilvania Company and *Lumby*[2] that wait upon him, and I fancy next Coll. Nicholson and perhaps—Ld. Corn. affaires, those Law Suits may go a good way to engage him upon this Voyage. However I hope the man that knows him to ye Bottom will tread hard upon his heeles, or close at least, if you there apprehend any mischief.

I have in mine by Burnam and in my last by Guy, or that Ship at least been Cargo to Several of thine, and therefore Shall only tell thee that thine of 7th 1*mo*. 1703-4, 29*th* 3*mo*. 1704, 30*th* 3*mo*. 1704, 27*th* 5*mo*. 1704, 25*th* 6*mo*. 1704, 4*th* 8*mo*. 1704 *and* 6*th* 2*mo*. 1704, 30*th* 3*mo* 1705 came alsoe to hand which saving that I have mentioned, I have answered. I lament the Separation of the Province and Counties; and I affirm I never intended So, but upon Condition I lost my Governm't and then that ye Countyes—as well as Province Should have the Same freedome.

[1] Had been a lawyer in Lewes, Delaware.

[2] Quarry, as judge of the admiralty court in 1699, had condemned the ship Providence of Stockwith, Capt. Lumby, because it had not been registered.

After the sale of the cargo, one-third of the proceeds was offered to Penn as proprietor, which he declined to use, and notified the owners of the vessel that it was at their disposal. Quarry and the advocate Moore were considered to have acted dishonorably in the case.

But the Lower Countyes were soo much the Occasion of all this Confusion, I fear by adhearing to ye Enemys of the Province, Quary, Moor, those villanous vipers. And it pleases me not a little, to find thee So apprehensive of their practises, and that thou hast made So great a part of the best of the Church People Sensible of their Base—and unreasonable designes. Not but that D. L. (one of ye worst of men) envying Moor, as folks of a Trade use to do, as well as Moor—leading him they may by begrudging —— Loyd his large practice among our Frds hath contributed to our Confusion. I have not yet *presented the Queen any of the Addresses Sent me*, because signd by a person *So obnoxious as D. L.*[1] and I am discouraged from it on that Acct. As for the Laws if the Fleet stays but 14 days longer, what are allowed Shall be Sent and *a letter from the Lords Comissioners for Trade and Plantations that will not disgust thee.* No Surrender yet, but when done (if done) depend upon it, I shall make it my Care for myself as well as thee, to Secure ye Governrs place for thee. The old Keeper is out, and William Cooper will be declared to morrow, and changes after that manner else where are expected which I hint for thy Aime. *Coll. Quary with his Protector Perry* have been with me, professes all fairness and friendlyness, and though thou didst not take his advice in proceeding agt the Vessell in an Admiralty way, yet he will only ask ye opinion of the Comissioners of ye *Customs for information and not complaint.* I know the Lords of Trade will drop it, and that of the Wool if not press, for they were pleased ye New-Englanders came at the Wool of Road Island [2] so ingenuously as they did 2 years ago by sheering of them on Connetticutt Side. *But complaint came to me from Philadelphia against ye increase of publick*, and the high rates *of* 8 *per c. Licence yearly which at* 50 *of them* Comes to 400£ per Ann. And they say it is more than twice the value of what they have or give here for them. I called to-day at thy mother's, but she was not at home, is well. So thy Friends Salute thee, *much is said of the Lewdnes of Pennsylvania. I beg of thee to have regard to my Character*, and give not that advantage against me either with God or good or bad men whose ill use of it I most fear, on a publick acct. I have just now Rec'd thine of 5th 5mo. (July) and am very Sorry that wicked man D. L. could blow up any of his Mermidons to such a pitch of brutishness as thy Acct. of William Biles[3] relates that is a meer vox et

[1] David Lloyd was born in 1656 in Manoron, co. Montgomery, Wales. Is said to have studied under Judge Jeffries. Arrived in Pennsylvania, in 1686, in ship Amity. A Quaker from policy and not principle it is thought, occasioned by his marriage in the province of Grace Growden, a superior woman. The last twenty years of his life he resided in Chester. He was chief-justice of Pennsylvania, and died at the age of 78, in 1731.

[2] The wool act of England punished with imprisonment and the loss of the left hand the sending of live sheep out of the kingdom, and no encouragement was given to the dressing of skins, or to manufactures in the colonies.

[3] William Biles was a prominent member of the council. He had come to Pennsylvania before Penn, and had settled on the Delaware river under a grant from Governor Andros. His plantation is marked on a map of 1679-80. He had a contempt for Evans and had used these expressions concerning him: "He is but a boy." "He is not fit to govern us." "We will kick him out." He and his wife were preachers.

praeterea nihil, a Coxcomb, and a Prag-matick in graine. That fellow's plantation is a Robbery upon Pennsbury, and, if there be a grant, was not a purchase from me, nor any Towed Land writs, for it was surveyed long before and done in my absence, formerly, and Judge Mompresson[1] can tell if I may not be deceived, in my Grant as well as the Crown, be it King or Queen,—Since, if confirmed, it was upon Surprize, and rattle an Inquisition about his eares, if not a prosecution. And know that when the time is expired of Session he may be taken to task, Since the Service he may pretend he was to attend is over. And first complain to the Friends, and if they wont or cant bow him to make Satisfaction, take it by Law thy Selfe. Pray mind what I say, be Secret, which is discreet, and fall on him or any other such unruly People at once, and make Some one Example to terrifie the rest. Thou hast not only my leave, but liking and encouragement whether called Quakers or others.

I hope yet to weather my difficulties here and there, and I hope what I Sent pr J. Guy 3 or 4ms. ago to testifie my case about the Laws, and in case of a Surrender, of their Priviledges, every way will deeply affect the honest hearted to be thankful and grateful. I have told thee of Coll. Q's discourse and professions before Mercht Perry and Some of our Friends and Shall watch his Steps. I pretty well ken and Shall watch him. Do you that are my good Friends there, your part to compose and maintain my just cause there, and I hope with God's assistance to prevent our Enemies here. I long since told J. Logan I wanted a Duplicate of the Laws, those Sent under ye great Seal, being presented to the Lords, and so out of my power, but as I occasionally borrow them. Howbeit almost ½ of them are demur'd to, as I have—already observ'd Perhaps by this opportunity I may say more about them, I could have those that are approv'd to Send presently but all ye Laws being under one Seale they Scruple having them presented by parcells and they cant present tho body but the rest will receive the Queen's Negative, and then they cease and you will be thereby difficient in Governm't; So that I am at a Stand, whether it may not be best to let them rest as they are, till those excepted agt *are amended*, wording them more properly being the greatest reason for the Attorney Genl and Lords Exceptions. Wherefore if the approved by the Lords go no farther, it is to Save the rest till they come in fuller Termes to be approved also. My Toyle and expensive daily Attendance with a boy to wait on me and a Scribe to Assist me at above 40 pr Ann. besides lodgings and food &c. are well known here even to great Streightness. How I can do more and Serve them better I dont know. The Lord uphold my life to my poor Family under all my troubles. Among many that ask

[1] Roger Mompesson is thus described by Penn in a letter to Logan: "He is a moderate churchman, knows the world here, has been in two several parliaments and recorder of Southampton, only steps abroad to ease his fortune of some of his father's debts." Was a favorite of Earl of Clarendon and proved worthless.

for thee *Sr. Roger Mosson* [Mompesson] *is one*, 'twas yesterday and remember to thee, and was not displeased at the Acc^{t}. I gave him.

Our heats here are great, and the mightiest party making that has been known, So that it Seems the Crisis of affaires and what way they take now is like to be lasting for the future. I beseech God to prevent farther breaches. Ch. Lawton is and all is well. Sr Jos. Fredenham dined there this week and myself. He has writ he tells me and will by this opportunity. For *my Son he has now writ to thee*, and other persons more largely than he did to me when there. He is like to be Somebody here in a while I think. Is glad,—with my Selfe, that there Seems a returne to me and my abused Interest, indeed to Justice, and Self preservation, among our Friends there, through the Example of those y^{t} were always reasonable in their thoughts and inclinations, pray cherrish and Smile upon Such and frequent and be easy and friendly with them totally to recover and establish them. *Birely is Arriv'd* mightily requested by *Ld. Cla. and Ld. Rochester*, not to appear against Ld. Corn. if that will do.

There's no certain news of ye taking of Barcelona, but there is certainly a Great revolt in Catalonia in favour of Ch. 3^{d}. but thou'lt have this and much more from ye com'n prints, to wch I refer thee. I shall be glad to hear of the good effects of ye opening of Trade with ye Spaniards and of your unanimity this Assembly for the publick good. Give my love to all our Sincere hearted Friends, whether Magistrates or others and let 'em know I have delay'd my Surrender on purpose, till the Laws that concern their Security are confirmed tho' reduc'd to great difficulties for want of Consideration I may justly expect thence. When thou hast occasion to write to the Ld of Trade or Com'issioners of the Customes inclose thy Letters to me that I may Second them.

I think I shall hardly Say much more at present But that I am with real affection

Thy faithful Fr^{d}.

WM. PENN.

[FROM THE SAME TO THE SAME.]

London 7th 12 mo. 1705.

Honoured Friend,

I did in my last inform thee, of what Letters I Rec'd. from thee; Since which came that of the 22^{d} Augt. the last before being of 5th of July as thy dates express. I am truly glad thy state of health returns thy great usefuleness to me engages me to desire and hope it and my Friendship not less, and as it is pleasing news to all thy Friends.

I sent thy Mother and friend Lawton theirs, who are with the rest of thy Friends well and salute thee. Mine are also I bless God, with the addition of another boy, now five in all, and with their Mother at their Grandfathers at Bristoll. Our laws are before the Queen, and what cannot be done at onse must be done at twise; for I will take the confirmation as I can get it. J. Logans last was of 9th 9br that by the Nonsuch is not yet come to hand nor Ld. Cornberrys 2 days ago, the lesson Letters are come to hand, which I admire at. So can send no answer.

Things go smooth with the Queen, as to home and foreign business and in Spain by Ld. Peterboroughs letter to me (who succeeds so far that most of Valentia and Arrogan have declared for the new King Charles the 3rd) who has made him Generallissimo of all his Armies every where, I have a letter from him of 2d, 9mo last, too days after the Secretarys and if the Recruits sent him, get time enough that King will in all probability, be in possession of Spain in a years time. For my surrender I govern myself by the dealings I find among you towards me. If I may believe Coll. Quary he goes highly Desposed to favour our affaires, words and his had, before divers, have pledged performances and I cannot perceive here otherwise, he sees how it is with me and that it will not hurt his interests to befriend mine, and a little time after his arrival if thou &c. think it for my advantage that he comes into the Counsil, he is willing, and I should be so too and that he be first or Second thereof to show he is reconsiled.

I wait ye Conclusion of the last Assembly, finally to take my own measures, and I hope to have it by the Pacquet not yet come to hand. I cannot at this distance Judge, but must depend upon thy judgmt and my best friends and time, and again ye people would not have me to do so, if not done, pray agree what I have to do and send it me pr. first I will loose no opportunity the inclosed is the Original of wt I sent of 7m and 8m last, by our last opportunity, fear not my regards to thee. I hear by Coll. Quarys Pacquet that is arrived pr. Nonsuch that the lower Countys have granted 1d pr pound, I hope ye Province will in no wise come behind them the continuation whereof would make our wheels go the faster, and you then get fresh heart. I know thy natural abilitys, and acquired address, and hope to feel the good effects thereof. I send thee a new Com'ission wt that Bullbegger left out of reservation to me or my Heirs in Legislation lodging that in thy brest of Integrity, which I rely upon, for that was made a mighty thing of. I hope thou keeps a good Correspondence wth Coll. Seymour and next neighbour because of Marylanders claim that I hope is more vexatious than hurtfull. I shall press the runing of the line, as I have done, and so no fault of mine it has not been before, but I know not what James Logan means by securing against ye Crowns pretentions as to the Boundaries. I have writ him of my private affairs and I hope his Zeal honesty and good Service, will keep him firme, and his own prudence in a due temper to give them acceptance with the concerned. In all occasions Show an utmost care not to offend on the side of the Queens Revenue, and the Just bounds of Admiralty authority. Coll. Quary has promised great moderation, and prays thou wilt take him with thee in those things, that so all occasions of misunderstanding may be prevented. I have writ also largely to our Frds. that writ so copiously to me, and they and their Interest prevails in this last Election and Assembly.

My Sister, Cous. Pools, Cousin John from Dantzik, my own son and Self dined at my Son and Daughter Aubreys to day all well and salute thee Coll Quary going early to-morrow. I must close, leave much to him to discourse and advise, upon honour, for the Ships lye in the Downs, but not without the honest love and regards wishing thee the best Success, for thy own hon^{r} and interest as well as mine and am,

Thy faithful and affect. friend,

Wm. Penn.

Give my Salutes to all
our friends in Governm^{t}.
& profession as if named.
Vale.

[From the Same to the Same.]

London, 27$_{th}$ 3 mo. 1708.

Esteemed Fr'd

Since my last to thee 15$_{th}$ 3 moth by Capt Hamilton, I have not till 2 days agoe of y^{e} 28th 7^{br} 1707 r'cved one title from thee, tho' so necessary to both our affairs, as well to my Enemies contrivances agst my Property, as ye seditions agst y^{e} Goverm't by y^{t} lett'r thou wilt perceive y^{e} objections to thy conduct. Since wch by other folks lett^{rs} I have heard of an extreme false step ab$_{t}$ a law made at N. Castle to ye prejudice of the fundamentall right and claime of y^{e} Province ; viz't free and undisturbed passage to and from y^{e} Province, in my Patent, most pathetically worded, wch seemes to have united y^{e} sev^{ll} Partys agst thee, and me, in consequence upon a common interest wch indeed looks like a finishing stroke to thy unhappyness. However that is not all, for ye charge of a lewed deportm^{t} at Conostogoe is mightily aggravated, wth thy journey incognito to bring ye mother and daughter on their voyage, or at least journey to ye ship after soe much freedom with the latter, at least knowing of ye former's escapeing out of prison to ye loss of her creditors. Two such capitall breaches of God's commandm'ts, and y^{t} of ye debtoress directly in ye very eye of ye governm't, y^{t} all I have been able to prevent some of our fr'ds from goeing to Queen and Councill, with ye complaints from ye Assembly there, and rather quietly to lay thee aside after soe many years being in, wch is customary wth ye Queen or Councill to doe as in ye case of ye Duke of Ormond, Ld Cornberry &c. than [illegible] obstinate dispute to have such things exposed, as must have disabled thee from other services or Employm^{ts} y^{t} yet thou mayst stand fairly for. This I thought the best way and so some of thy truest and kindest frds to prevent y^{e} mallice of some ill Spirits. So y^{t} thou must give such a Proof of thy discretion as may bespeake thy Preferm't in some Station not Less beneficial.

Esqr Lawton, Parson Evans,[1] Netervill thy uncle & mot^{r} have been acquainted wth y^{e} reason of this, for no Long^{er} agoe than y$_{e}$ begining of this month 3 Persons who had rec'd y^{e} last as well as former Assembly's Invectives agst thee Came wth a sort of Impeachment from them there agst thee to y^{e} Queen, and made me their last Complaint, and if rejected to proceed to Queen and Councill; so y^{t} w^{t} we have done was y^{e} best y^{t} offered for thy advantage, some things being to likely to be proved, and by some upon ye Spott, y^{t} are of a very reprovable nature, and Injustice to my own character there and here, I could not any longer reject their request, to Change hands, and therefore I Petitioned ye Queen in these Termes, and y^{t} was all ye reason I gave for praying her approbation of my Choice and Commission.

Now know that I take thy care of my interst in Minerall matt^{rs}. very kindly, and shall certainly hold myself obliged if Mitchell[2] be made true, and y^{t} ye vallue rises as I have heard by J. Logan, &c. who I perceive by thine seems to guess rather than know. His on y^{t} subject was dated this moth a year or near it. Such an affair Judiciously, and as honestly Performed will quickly end my misfortunes, and enable me to doe wond^{rs} for y^{t} poor Country after all ye ingratitude as well as Injustice of some Perverse tempers in it, whome God forgive. I hope ye tenor of this Lett^{r} will not be able to provoke thee to either, but after w^{t} has been said, and reasons for it, rather quicken thee to recommend thyself to ye Services, I and mine here away may be able to rend^{r} thee in a future regard, and for ye New Castle people they may happen to find themselves mistaken at Last, I mean the Lower Countys busy folks y^{t} have not used me wth Justice or gratitude or Common Civility, but I committ my Cause to God agst all my unworthy Enemy's of whome R. Hallwell I have heard is y^{e} Greatest, time fails me, y^{e} bearer is sent for to Liverpool where y$_{e}$ Ship lyes he has taken a passage in, and sets out to-morrow early upon his Journey of wch I had no notice till to-day by himself, Lord Lovelace sailes in a month, and I think by him to write w^{t} I omitt now, and therefore conclude, wth y^{e} good wishes of me, mine, and all thy best frd's w^{t} I am and desire to be. Thy assured fr'd to serve thee when I may.

29. 4m. 1708.

I have yesterday thine of the 12 of 11mo. (Jan.) 1707-8, and I shall improve it the best I can with those warm'd ag'st thee, but it comes 2 months to late;

[1] Rev. Evan Evans came to Philadelphia in 1700, and was the preacher at Christ (the Episcopal) Church. After the first meeting of a presbytery in Philadelphia, he went to London in 1707, and urged the appointment of a bishop or suffragan for America. In his memorial he alludes to the recently formed presbytery in these words: "Wheresoever presbytery is established, there they have the face and appearance of an ecclesiastical jurisdiction and authority after their way, to resort to upon all occasions. But our clergy in America are left destitute of any advantages of this kind."

His connection with Christ Church terminated in 1719. Although a Welshman he was not a relative of the governor.

[2] See foot-note [1] on p. 5.

a publick war or a change of hands must be, and accordingly, Coll. Charles Gooking will succeed thee who will I hope give at least some content. He has commanded men, is about 48 years of age, and intends to Sow all he has in ye Country & become a planter & will waite on Lord Lovelace y^t goes in 3 weeks they say. I hope for a word about the —— thy last mentioned. Thy unckle brought thine yesterday, as well to thy Mother. Thy ff'ds wish thee well, but nobody more than

Thy reall ffriend

WM. PENN.

T. Grey is wth me & gives thee
his best respects. Endeavours me for
thy service here, by thy ff'ds.

www.ingramcontent.com/pod-product-compliance
Lightning Source LLC
LaVergne TN
LVHW020636110826
845149LV00004B/1235